Abandoned UK

Robert Nelson

Take only photographs // Leave only footprints

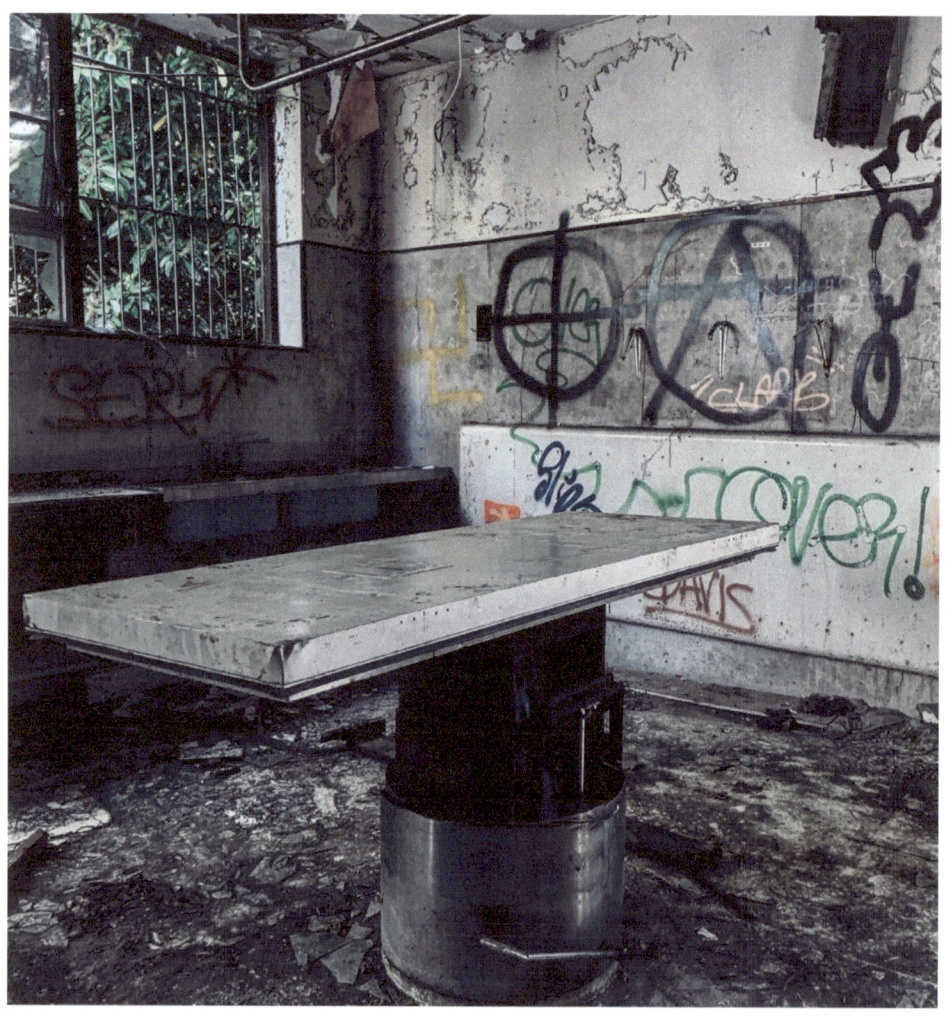
Body Slab in an abandoned Morgue.

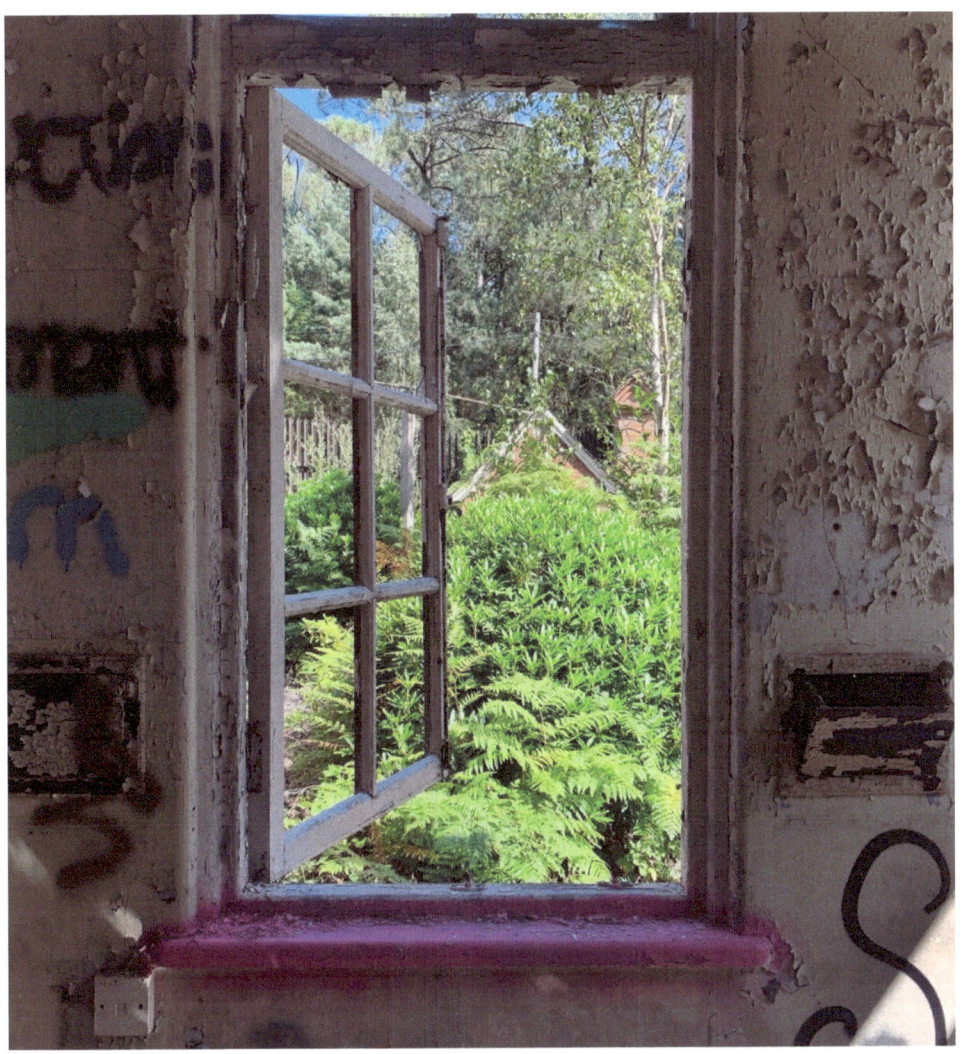

The view from a window in an office within an abandoned arms factory.

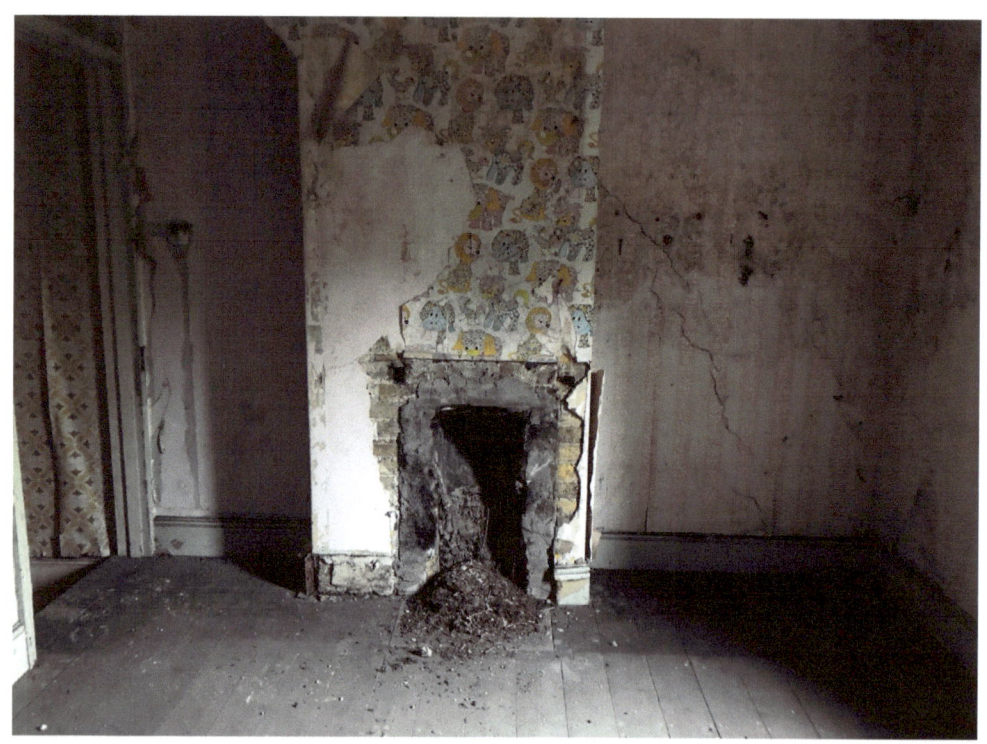
Fireplace in a house from the 1940's. Not lived in since then and now used for MOD training.

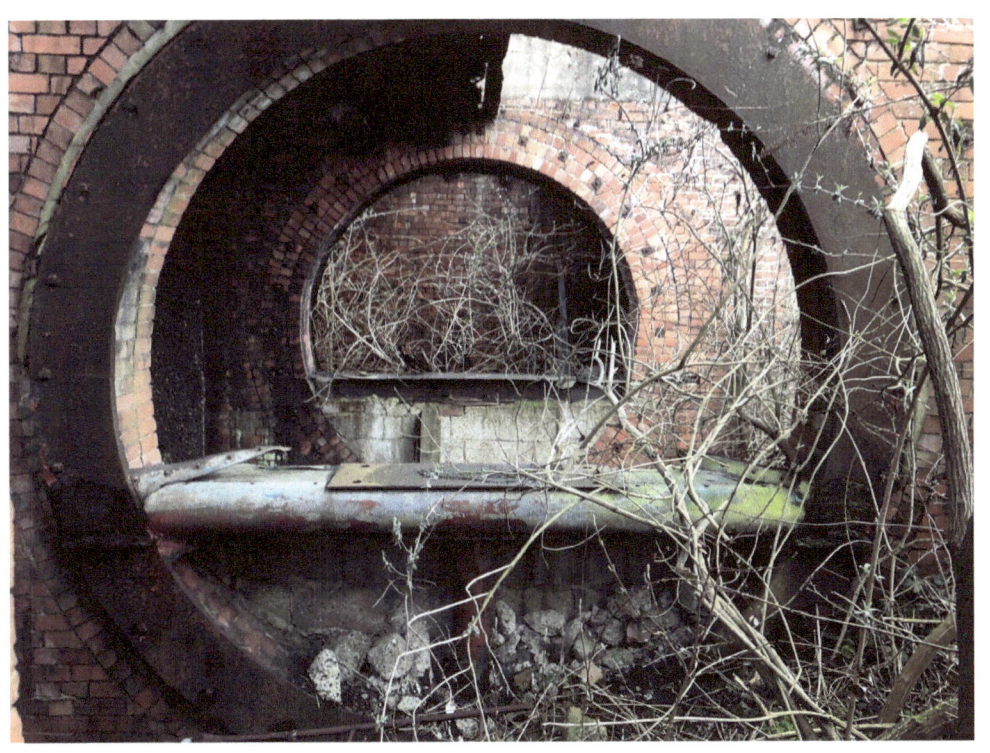
Abandoned factory.

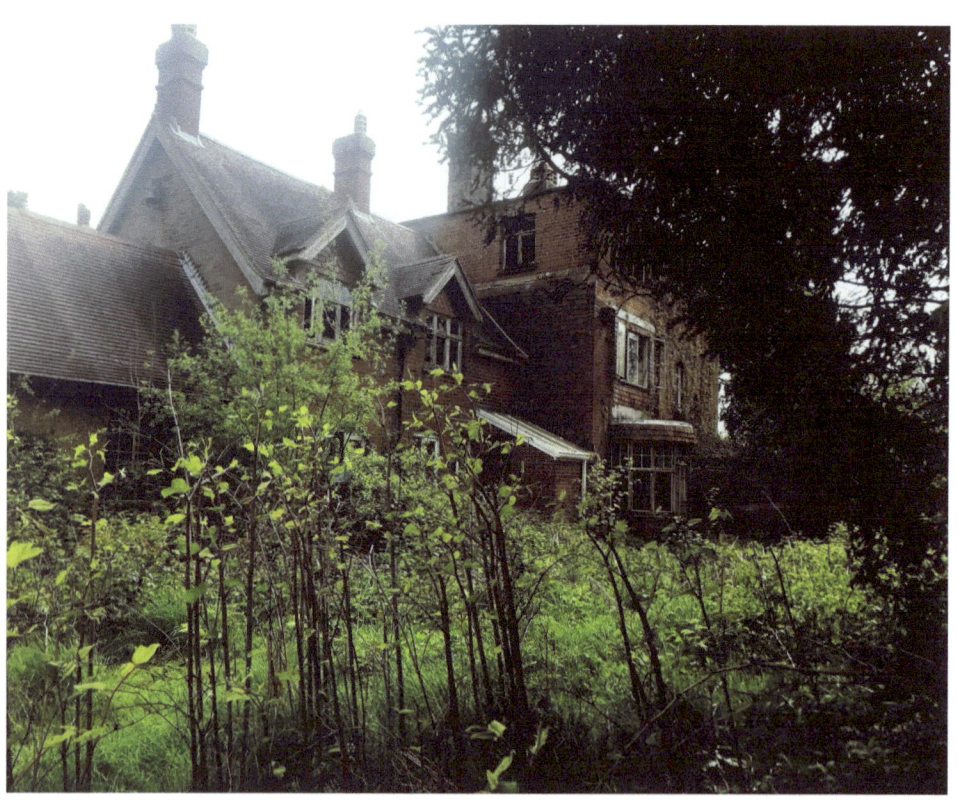

Abandoned Manor – once a hotel, then a war respite and finally a family home. Currently for sale.

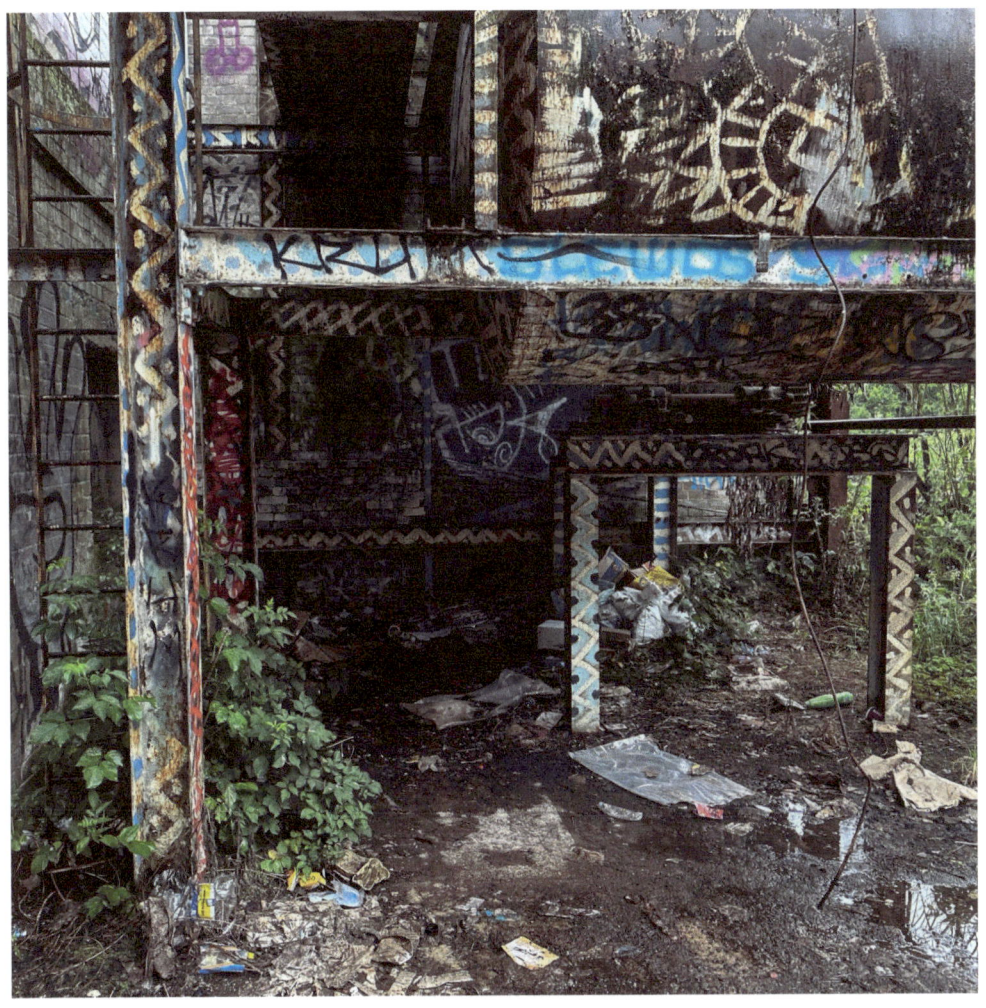
Abandoned lime works factory.

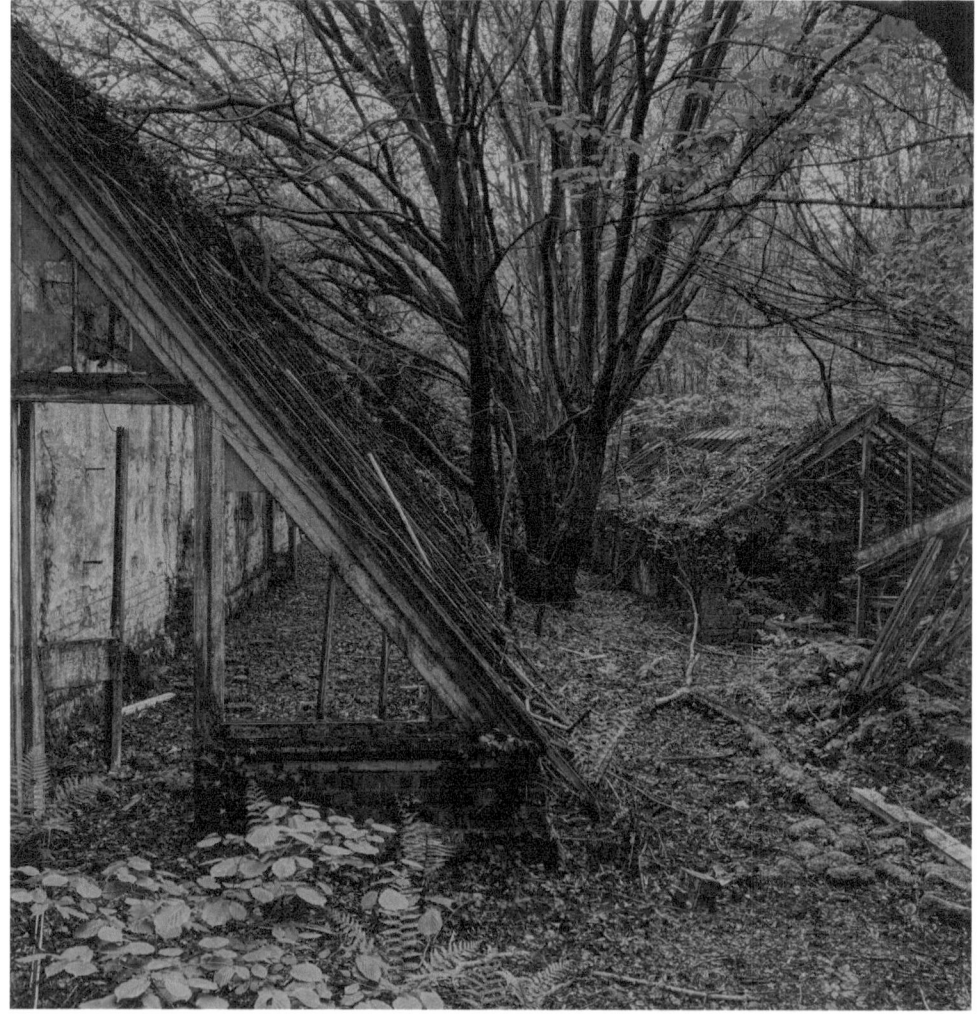
Abandoned garden on the grounds of a derelict part of an active hospital.

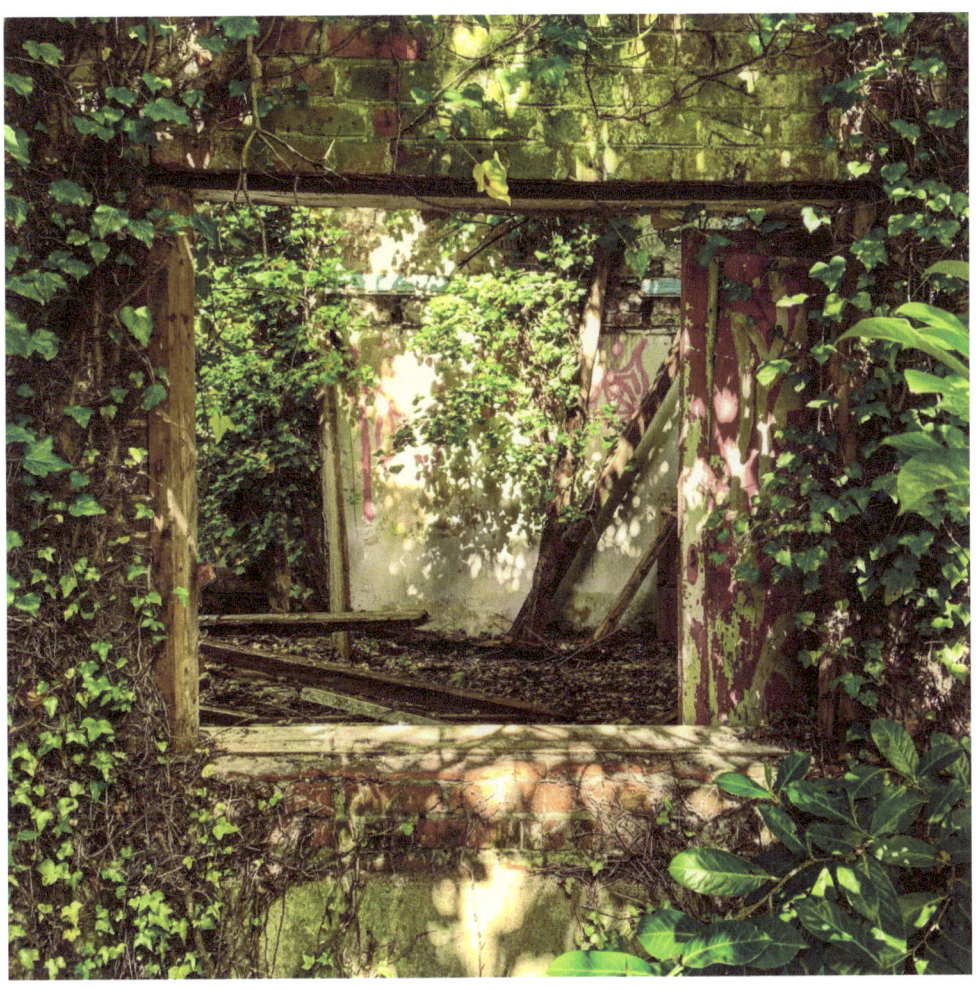
View from the window of an abandoned groundskeepers house on hospital grounds.

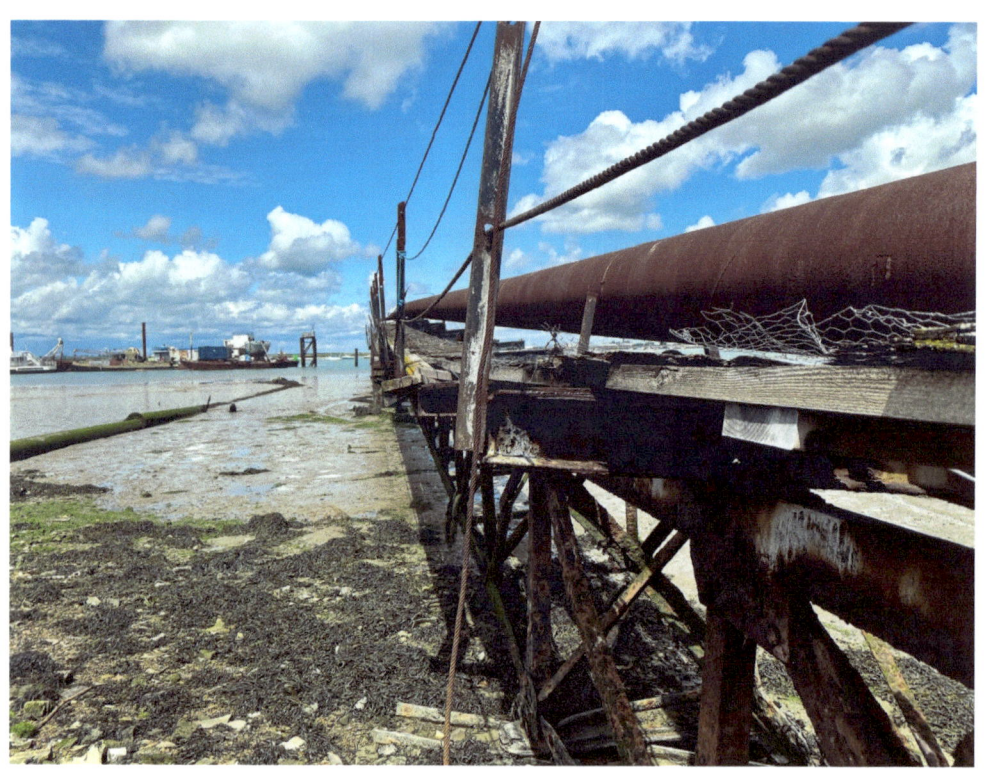
View from an abandoned dock.

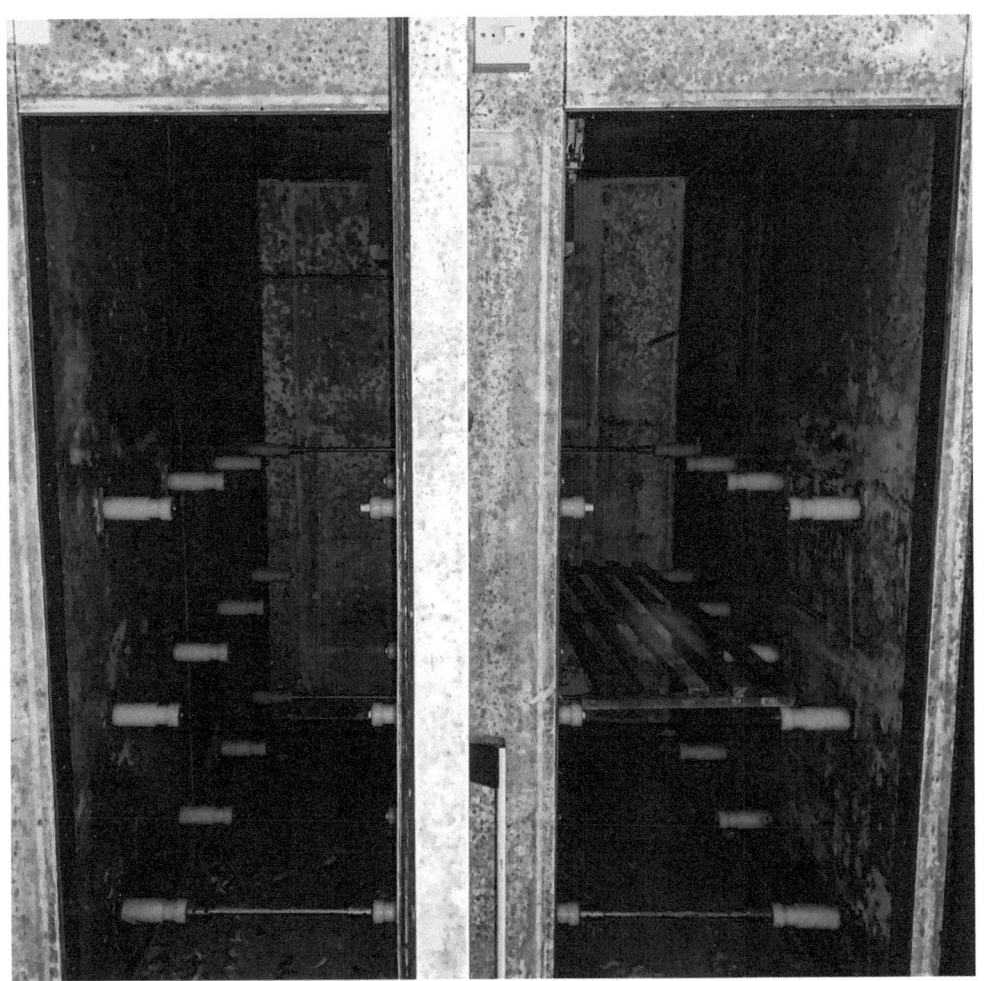

Cadaver locker. Basement of abandoned hospital.

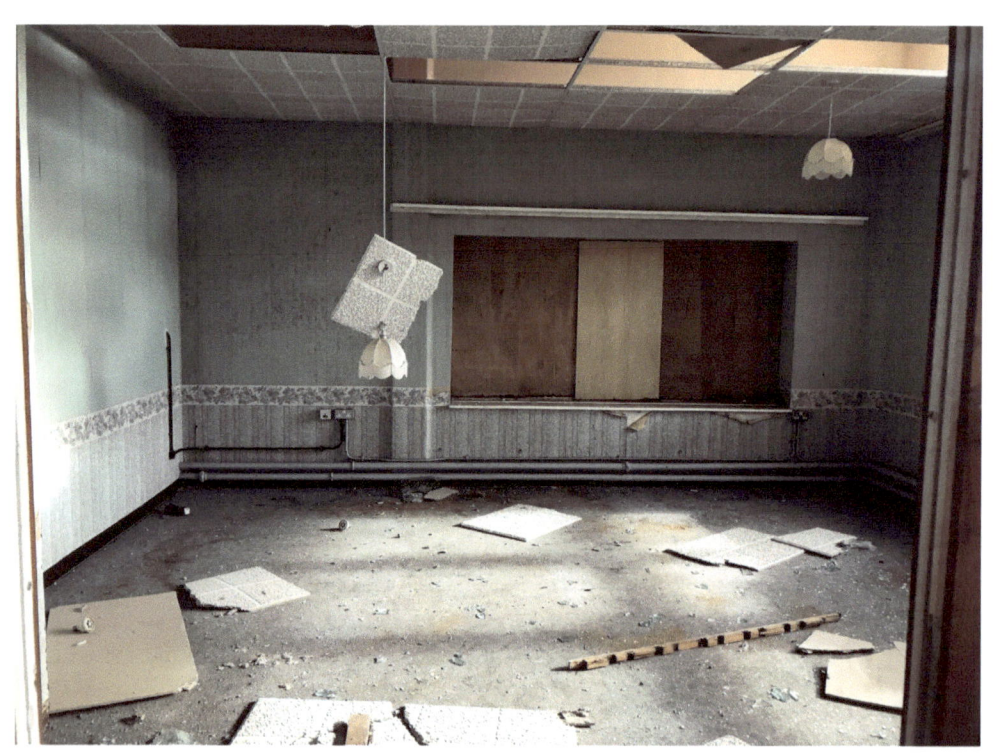

Waiting room – abandoned hospital.

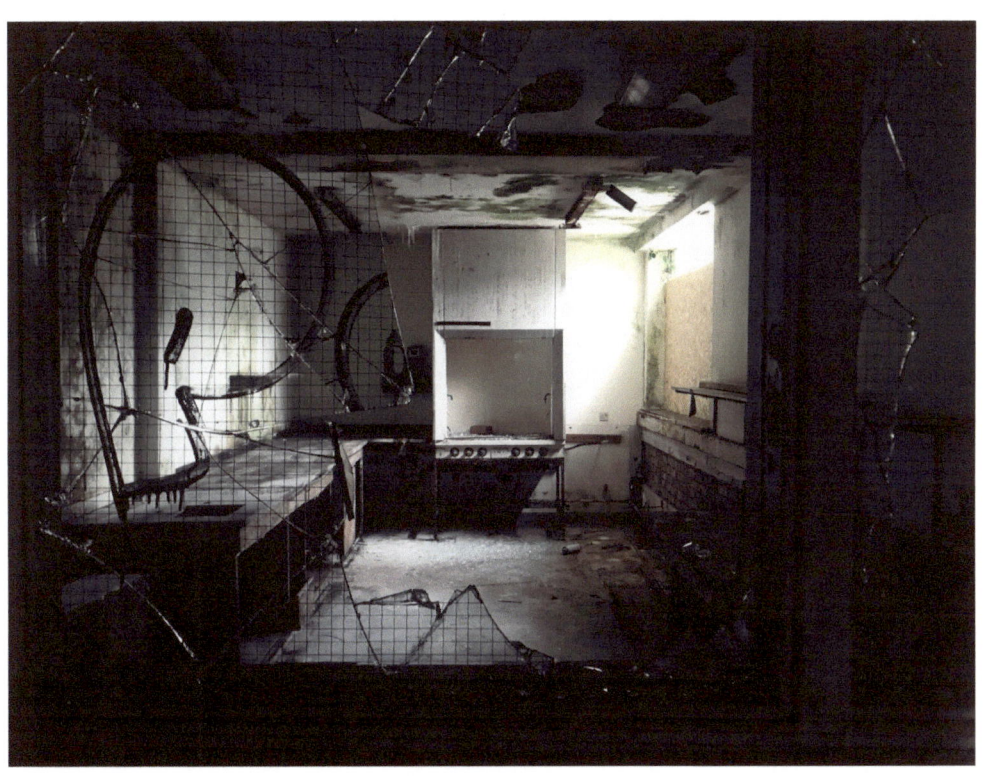

View from the door into an abandoned classroom.

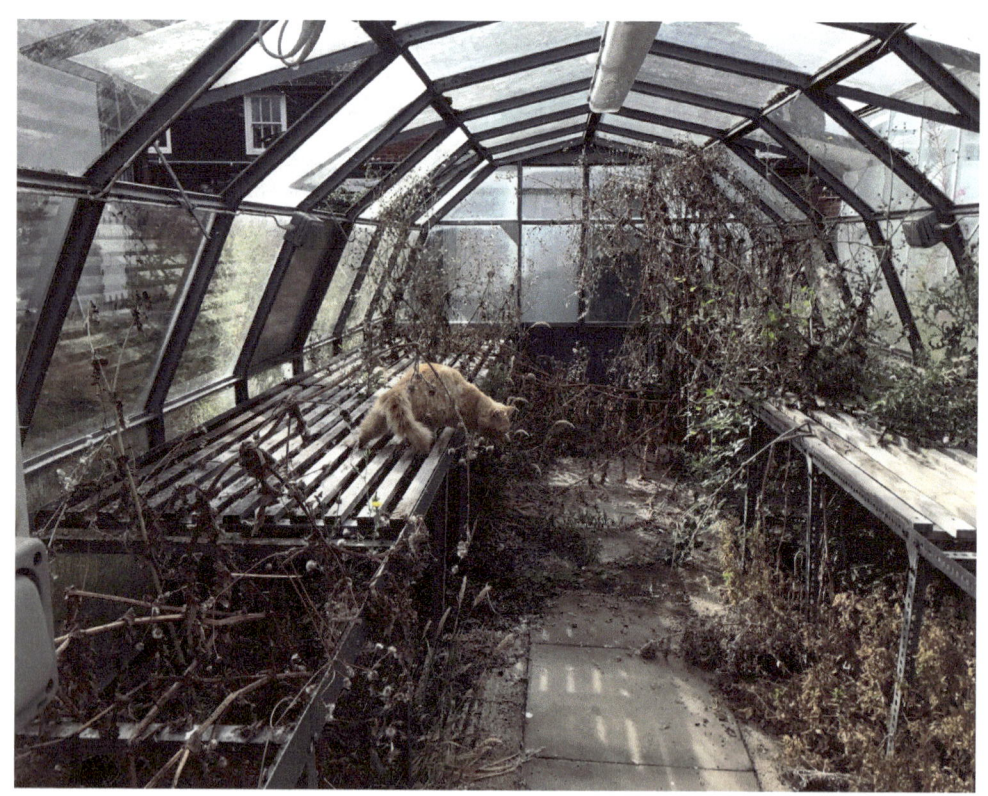
Abandoned greenhouse – university grounds.

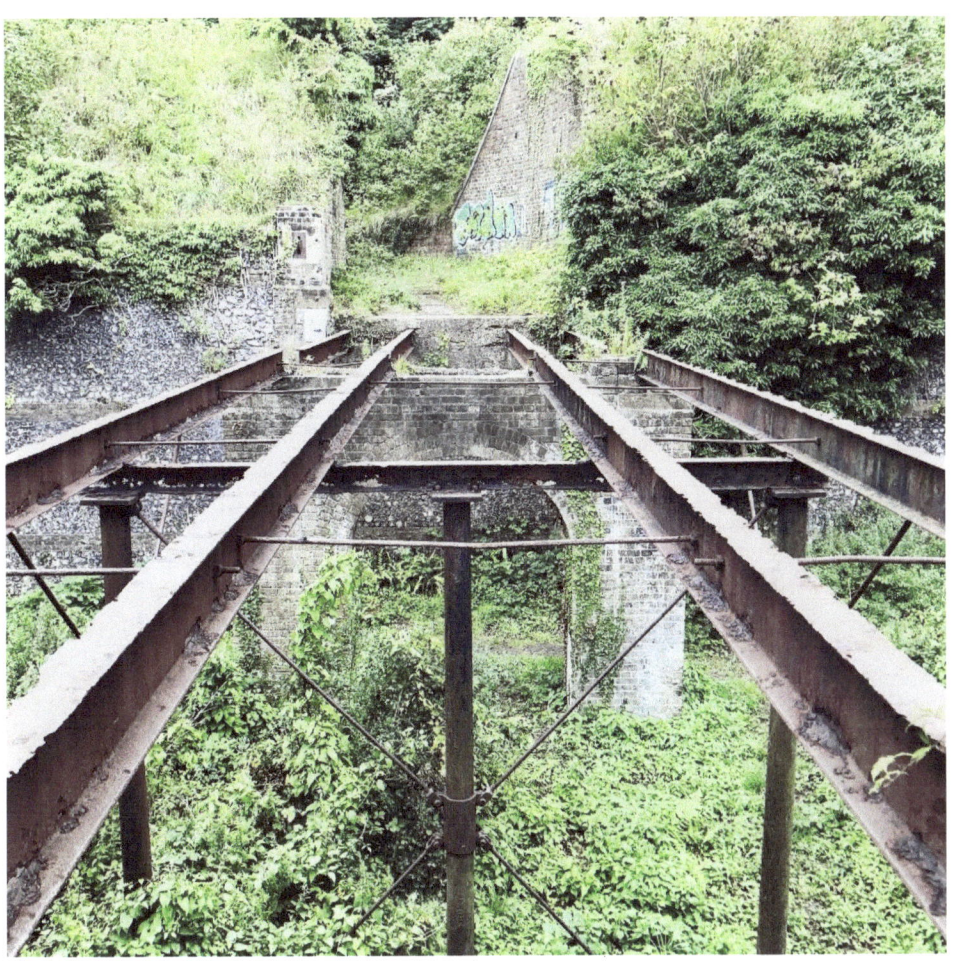
Decommissioned bridge – abandoned war fort.

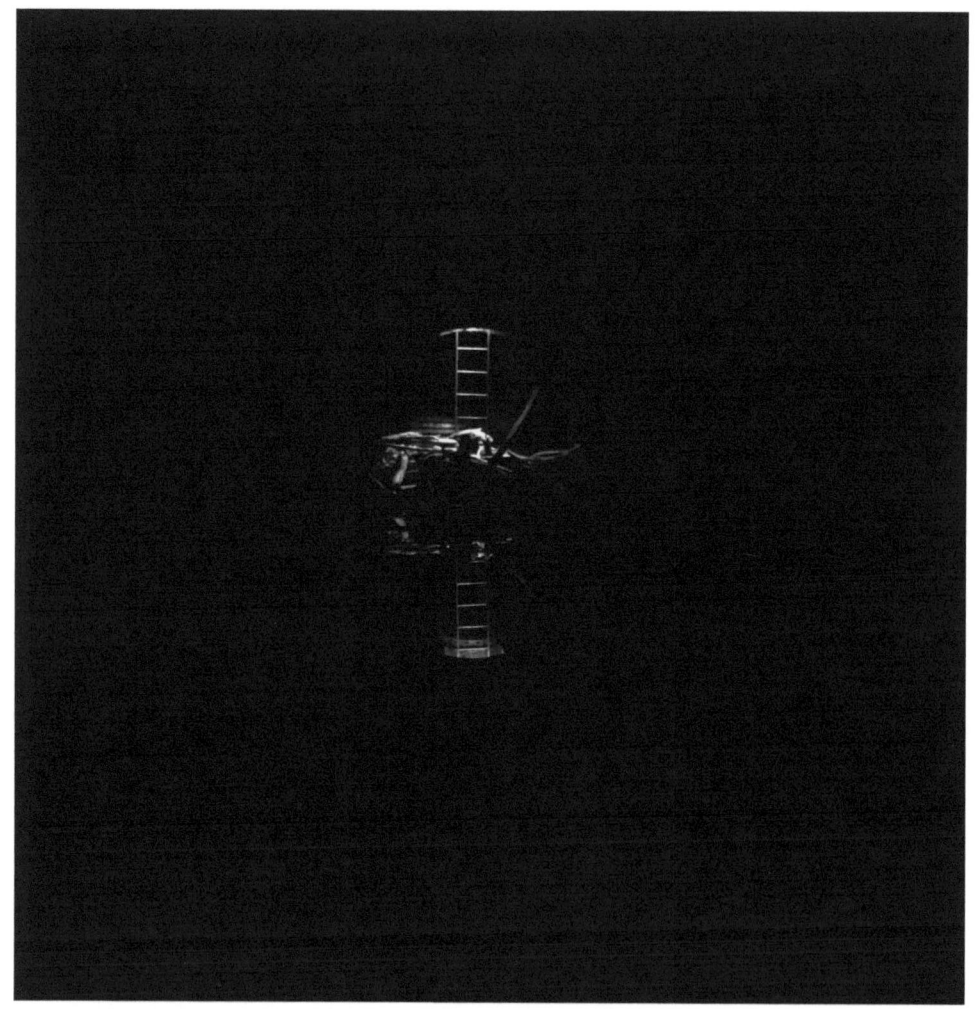

Underground war tunnel – flooded.

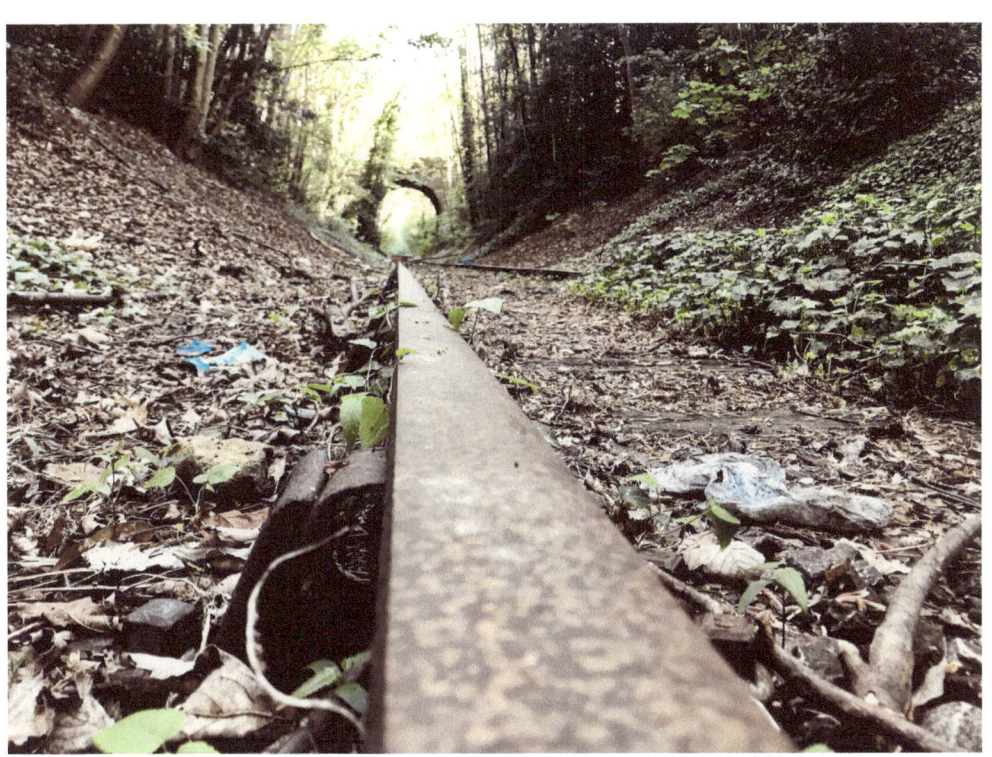
Decommissioned railway line.

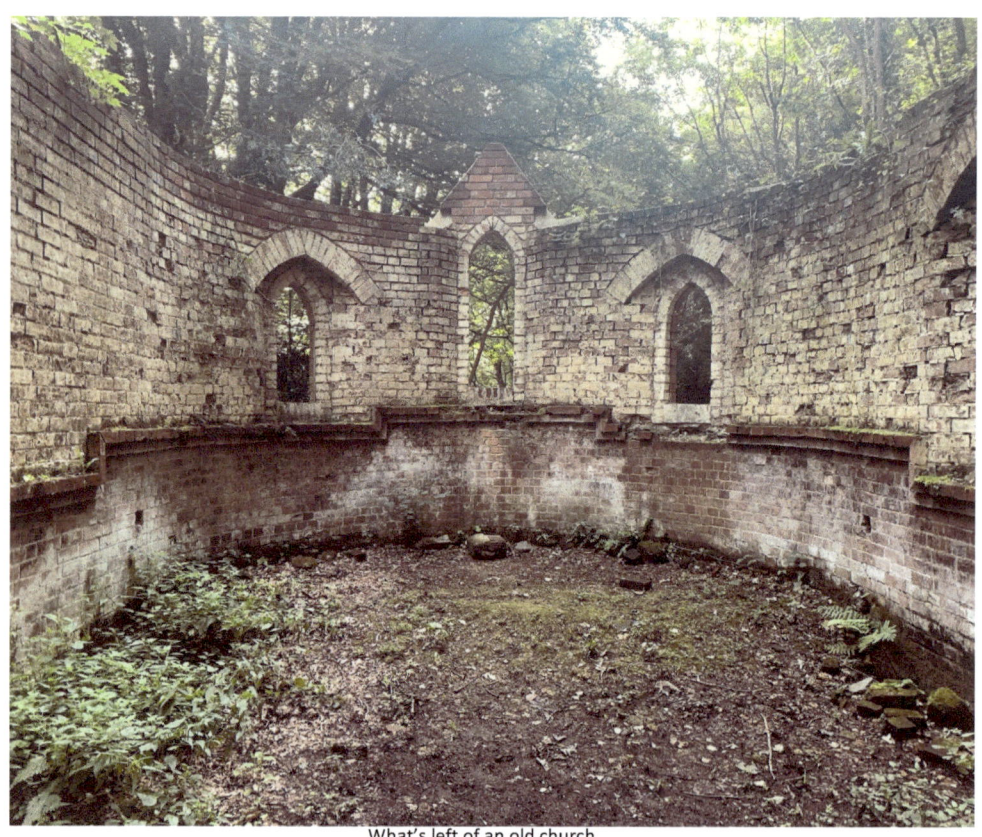
What's left of an old church

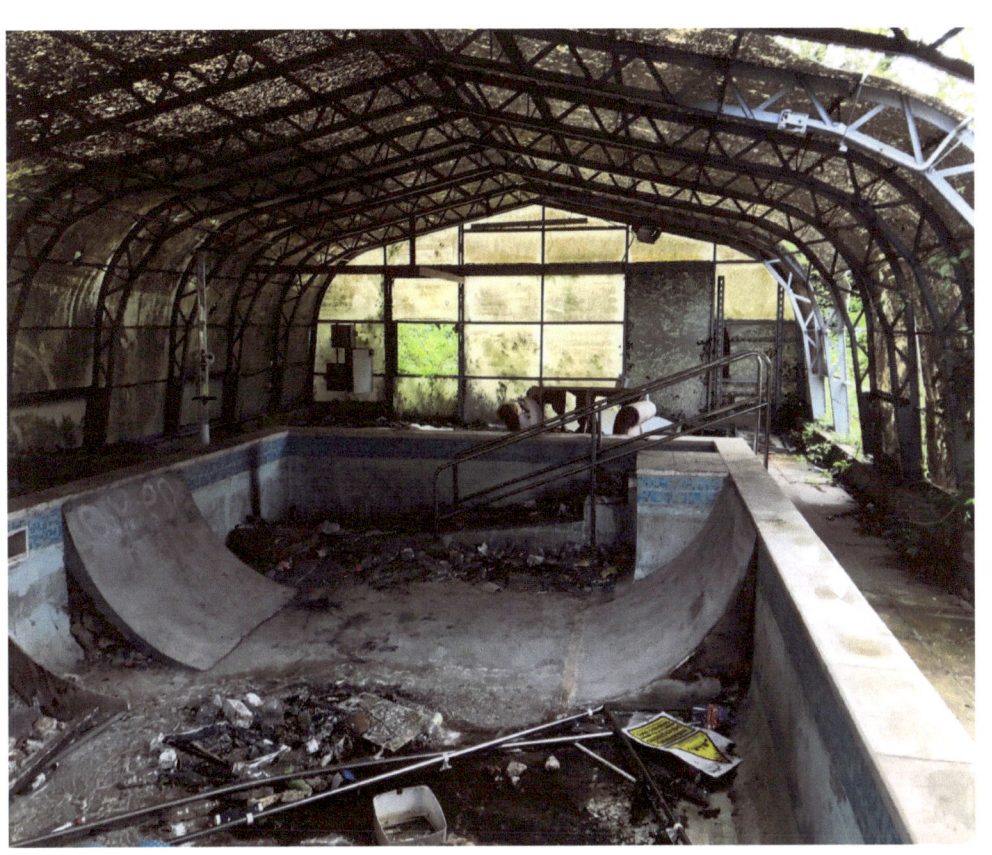
Swimming pool in abandoned school for disabled children.

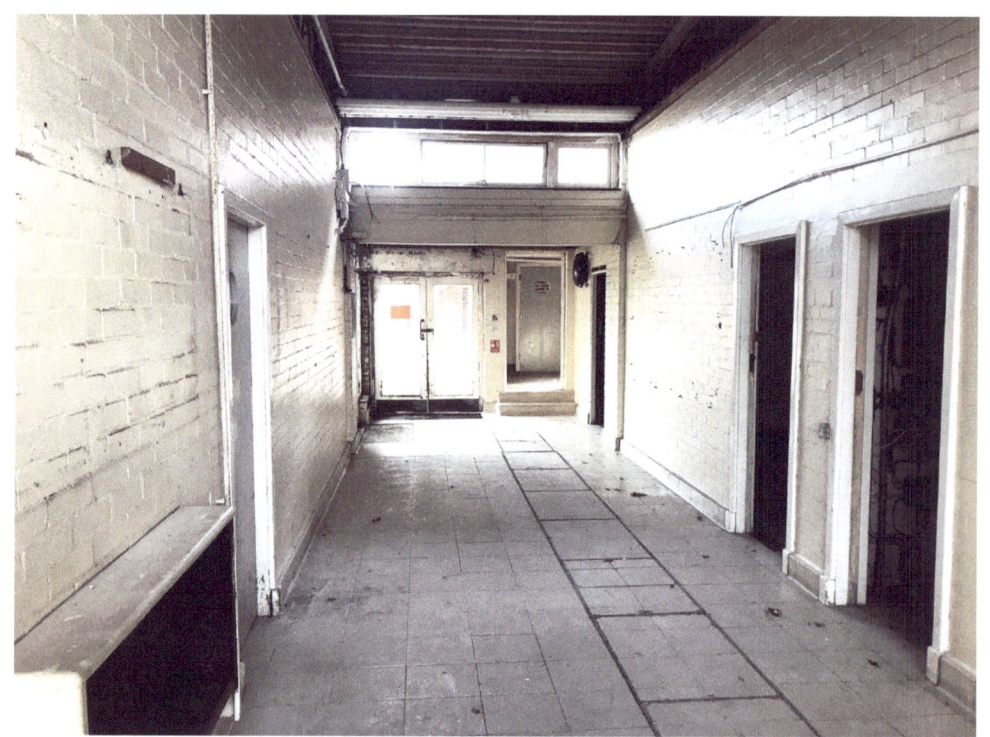

School hallway.

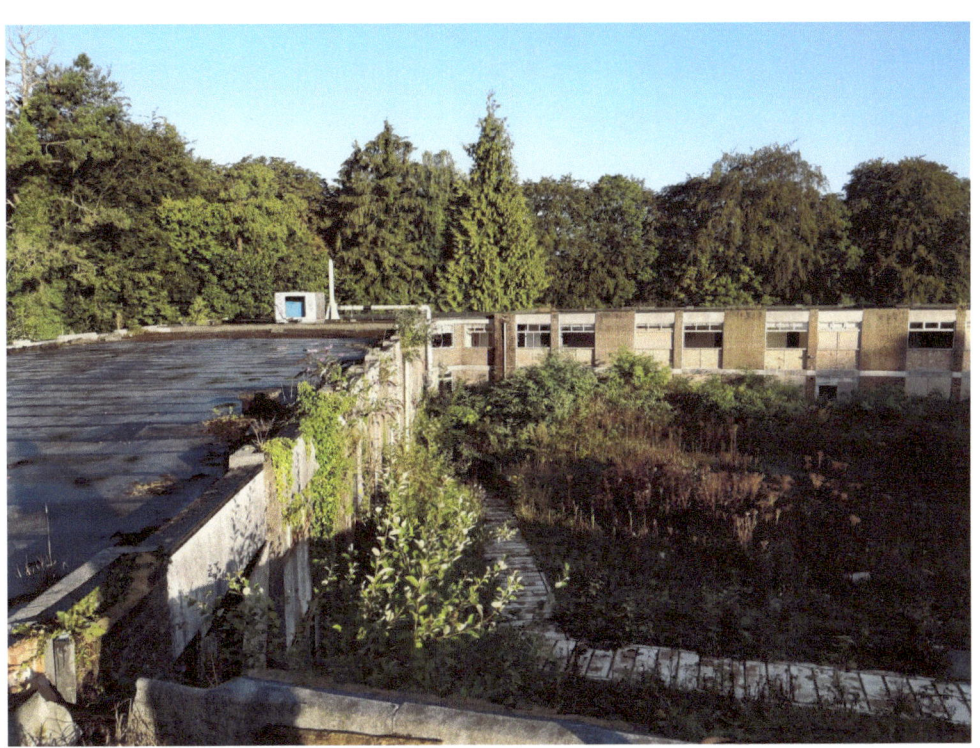
View from roof of abandoned laboratory.

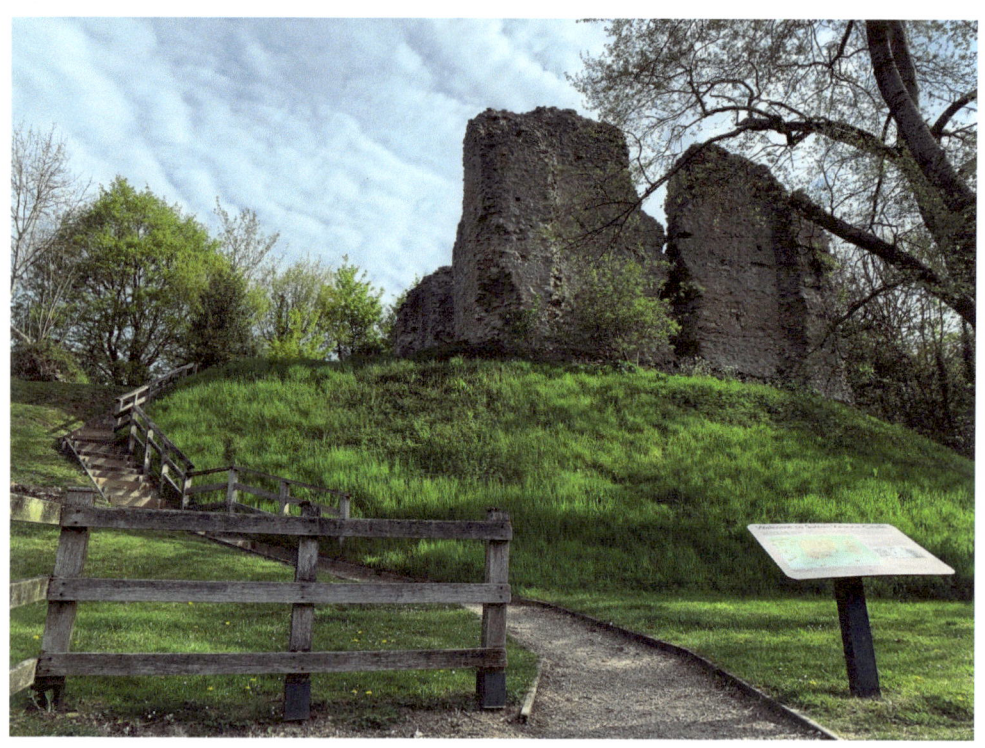
Abandoned castle – open to public. (Maidstone)

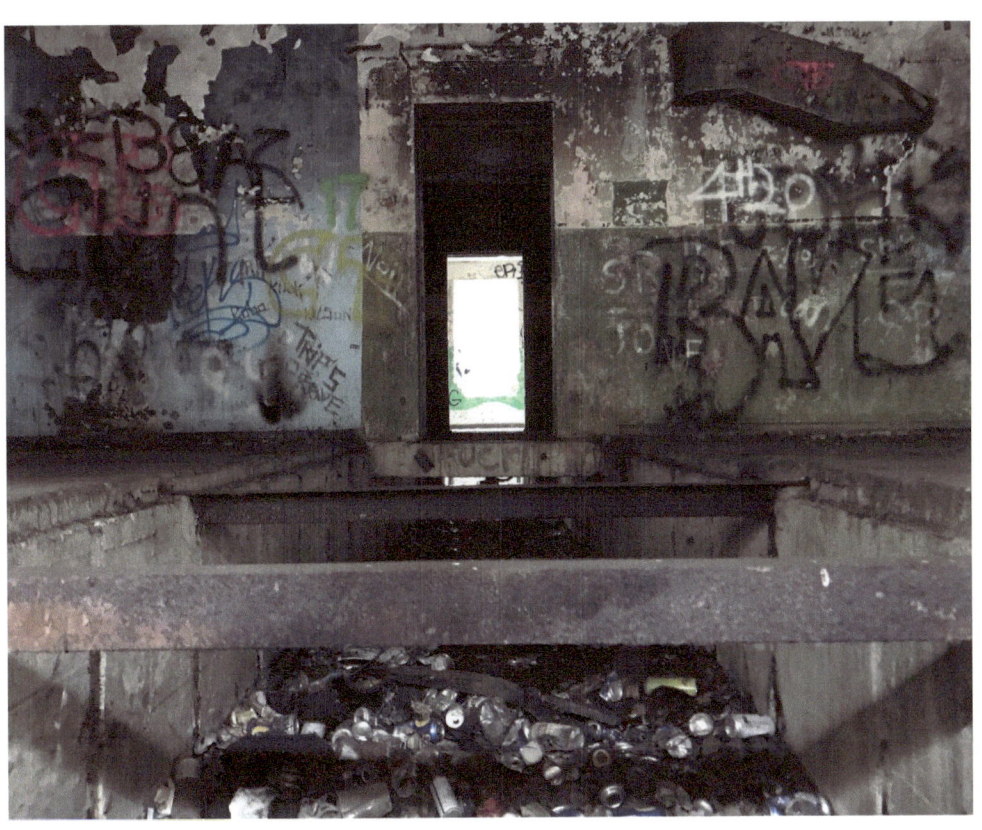

Inside an abandoned radio tower – used during WW2.

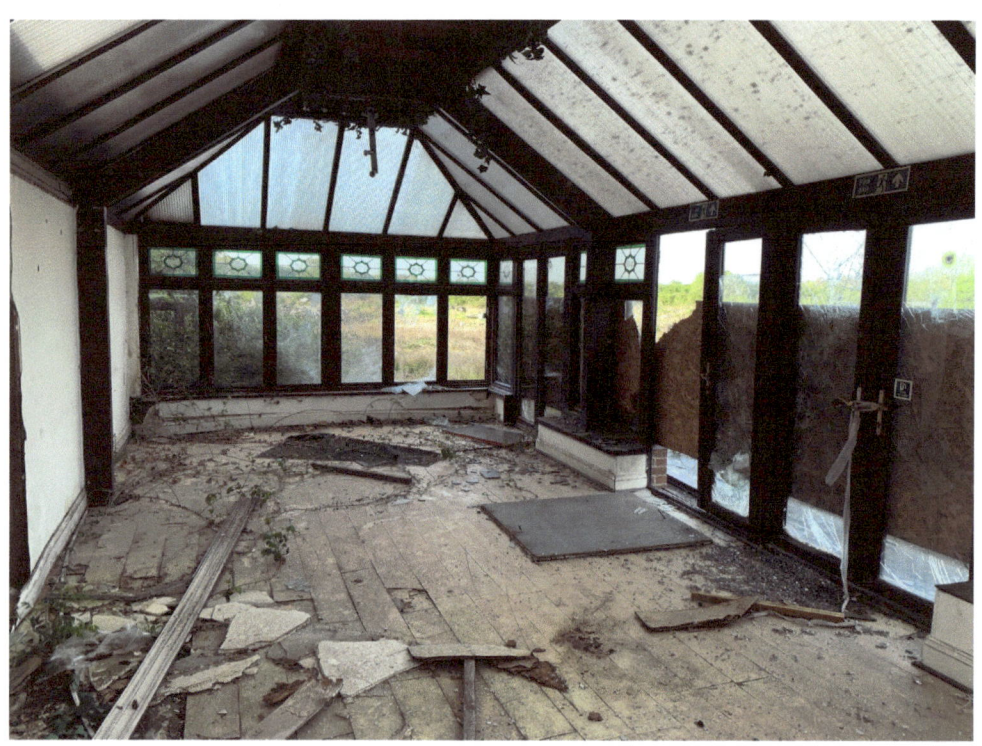

Abandoned restaurant dining room.

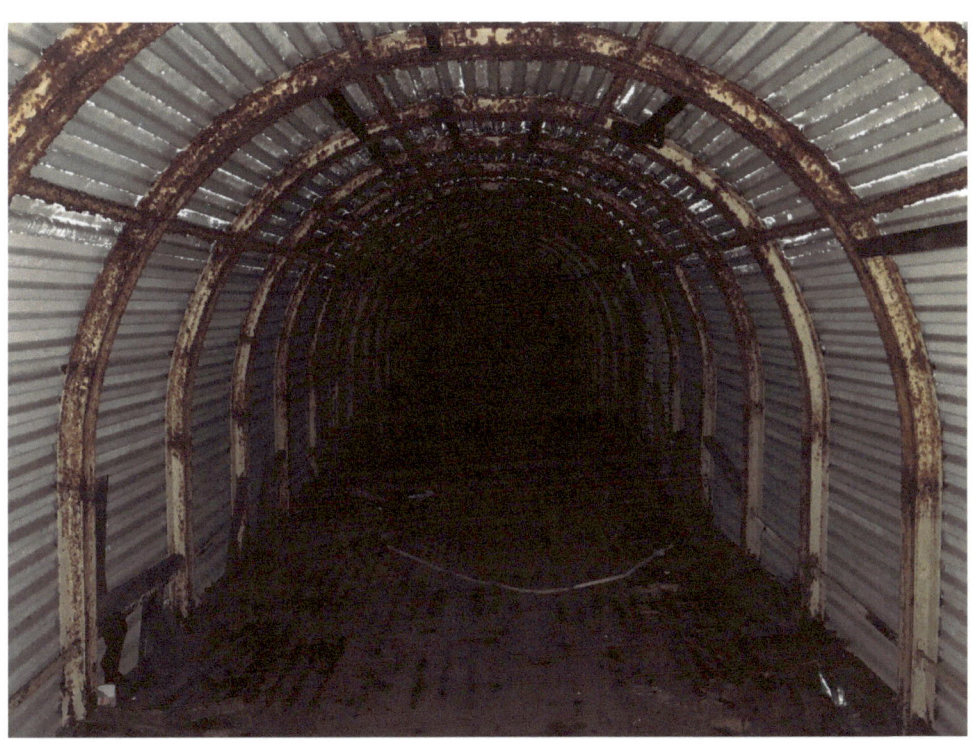
Inside an abandoned WW2 tunnel, used for transporting rockets.

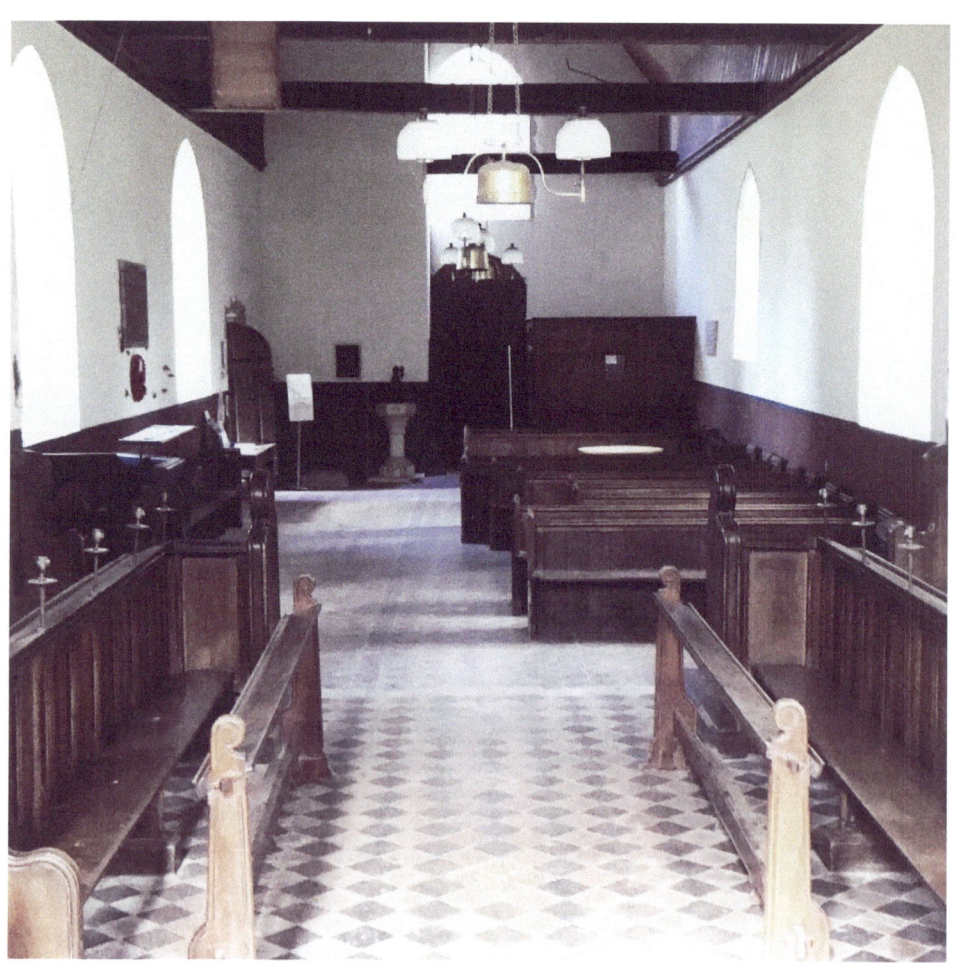

Abandoned Church.

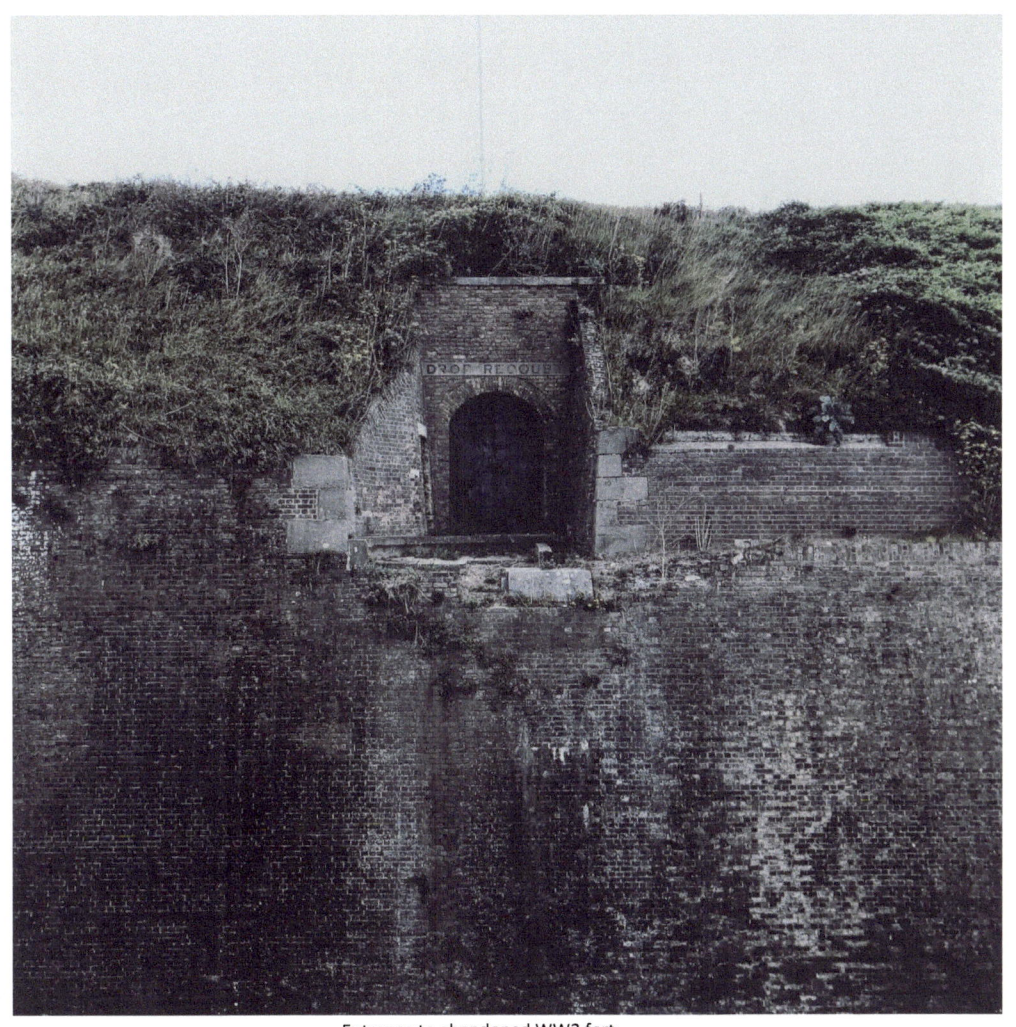
Entrance to abandoned WW2 fort.

Thanks for purchasing.

For more – visit Instagram, YouTube and Facebook and search Urban Xplore Kent.

www.ingramcontent.com/pod-product-compliance
Lightning Source LLC
Chambersburg PA
CBHW040347220526
45473CB00009B/2804